preteen Bible study series

# Getting Along With Others

Loveland, Colorado

## Group's R.E.A.L. Guarantee to you:

This Group resource incorporates our R.E.A.L. approach to ministry—one that encourages long-term retention and life transformation. It's ministry that's:

**Relational**
Because learner-to-learner interaction enhances learning and builds Christian friendships.

**Experiential**
Because what learners experience through discussion and action sticks with them up to 9 times longer than what they simply hear or read.

**Applicable**
Because the aim of Christian education is to equip learners to be both hearers and doers of God's Word.

**Learner-based**
Because learners understand and retain more when the learning process takes into consideration how they learn best.

**preteen Bible study series**

# Getting Along With Others

Visit our Web site: **www.grouppublishing.com**

**Credits**
Author: Mike Nappa
Editor: Jim Hawley
Creative Development Editor: Karl Leuthauser
Chief Creative Officer: Joani Schultz
Copy Editor: Larry Haise
Art Director: Kari K. Monson
Cover Art Director/Designer: Jeff A. Storm
Cover Photographer: Daniel Treat
Print Production Artist: Joyce Douglas
Illustrator: Shawn Banner
Production Manager: DeAnne Lear

0-7644-2468-8

10 9 8 7 6 5 4 3 2     12 11 10 09 08 07 06 05 04 03

Printed in the United States of America.

# Contents

Gateway Christian Church

# *Introduction:*
## *Getting Along With Others*

It was an odd combination, really. A rebel, a skeptic, a crooked tax collector, a member of the royal court, and several ignorant fishermen. Individually they weren't very impressive. However, joined in service to a carpenter-turned-preacher, they changed the world.

Your preteen group may contain a combination of students just as unusual as the first disciples. Yet banded together in service to Jesus, they, too, have the potential to impact the world for Christ's sake.

Unfortunately, preteens may find themselves limited by the stereotypes that prevail in our society. This study helps preteens overcome stereotypes based on race, culture, beliefs, and social status. The things kids experience through *Getting Along With Others* can help them develop open communication with all kinds of people and give them a sense of unity with other Christians. In the first study, they'll explore how God made each person unique and different.

> Your preteen group may contain a combination of students just as unusual as the first disciples. Yet banded together in service to Jesus, they, too, have the potential to impact the world for Christ's sake.

Next your students will learn the value of reaching out to people of other cultures. In the third study, preteens will explore strategies for overcoming racism and prejudice.

The last study will help students learn that Christian denominations all fit into the big picture of "church." This book will help preteens get along with others who are different from them—their friends, people in other cultures, or in different churches—as their emerging world of new relationships grows.

# About Faith 4 Life: Preteen Bible Study Series

The Faith 4 Life: Preteen Bible Study Series helps preteens take a Bible-based approach to faith and life issues. Each book in the series contains these important elements:

• **Life application of Bible truth**—Faith 4 Life studies help preteens understand what the Bible says, and then apply that truth to their lives.

• **A relevant topic**—Each Faith 4 Life book focuses on one main topic, with four studies to give your students a thorough understanding of how the Bible relates to that topic.

• **One point**—Each study makes one point, centering on that one theme to make sure students really understand the important truth it conveys. This point is stated upfront and throughout the study.

• **Simplicity**—The studies are easy to use. Each contains a "Before the Study" box that outlines any advance preparation required. Each study also contains a "Study at a Glance" chart so you can quickly and easily see what supplies you'll need and what each study will involve.

• **Action and interaction**—Each study relies on experiential learning to help students learn what God's Word has to say. Preteens discuss and debrief their experiences in large groups, small groups, and individual reflection.

• **Reproducible handouts**—Faith 4 Life books include reproducible handouts for students. No need for student books!

• **Flexible options**—Faith 4 Life preteen studies have two opening and two closing activities. You can choose the options that work best for your students, time frame, or supply needs.

• **Follow-up ideas**—At the end of each book, you'll find a section called "Changed 4 Life." This provides ideas for following up with your students to make sure the Bible truths stick with them.

Use Faith 4 Life studies to show your preteens how the Bible is relevant to their lives. Help them see that God can invade every area of their lives and change them in ways they can only imagine. Encourage your students to go deeper into faith—faith that will sustain them for life! Faith 4 Life, forever!

# Uniquely Me!

**The Point:** ➤ God made each of us unique and different.

Preteens pressure each other to fit into the "right" groups and cliques, or face being left out. Young adolescents learning the importance of friendships often will do whatever it takes to fit in.

Facing this reality, preteens at times cannot see the importance of recognizing and appreciating the unique qualities God has gifted each student with.

Use this study to help your students appreciate the differences between themselves and others, and to help them live up to their God-given potential.

## Scripture Source

### 1 Corinthians 12:12-27

Paul uses the analogy of the human body to describe how different people make special contributions to the family of God. He provides us with a physical picture that shows how Christians need each other. Just as the eye benefits from the hand and head needs the feet, Christians need each other and must work together to build a strong church body.

## The Study at a Glance

| Section | Minutes | What Students Will Do | Supplies |
|---|---|---|---|
| **Warm-Up** Option 1 | up to 10 | **Pick of the Litter**—Pick an imaginary pentathlon team. | Paper, pens |
| **Warm-Up** Option 2 | up to 15 | **Pyramid Building Challenge**—Work in groups to build different kinds of pyramids. | |
| **Bible Connection** | up to 15 | **Body Parts Relay**—Participate in a relay with blindfolds and compare the game to 1 Corinthians 12:12-20. | Bibles, blindfolds |
| | up to 15 | **Many People, One Body**—Match body parts with character qualities and explore 1 Corinthians 12:20-27. | Bibles, "Many People, One Body" handouts (p. 13), pens |
| **Life Application** | up to 10 | **Seeking the Unique**—List one unique thing about themselves. | Index cards, pens |
| **Wrap-Up** Option 1 | up to 5 | **Getting Along**—Write notes to people they want to get along with better. | Postcards, pens |
| **Wrap-Up** Option 2 | up to 10 | **Team Appreciation**—Tell other group members one special way they each contribute to the group. | Construction paper, scissors, markers, tape |

Set out Bibles, blindfolds, construction paper, writing paper, tape, markers, scissors, index cards, postcards, and pens. Also make enough photocopies of the "Many People, One Body" handout (p. 13) for each preteen.

# The Study

## Warm-Up Option 1

**Pick of the Litter** *(up to 10 minutes)*

*The Point* ➤

When preteens have arrived, **say:** Today we're going to explore how ➤God made each of us unique and different. Let's do a fun activity to see what this might look like with some famous people.

Form groups of no more than four. Give each group a sheet of paper and a pen. Have groups each select six famous people to be on a pentathlon team. The events their imaginary team must compete in are flag football, a baking contest, a round of Jeopardy!, a game of basketball, and an acting contest.

Have groups each choose their team members from real people, such as sports stars, actors, musicians, and politicians, and list them on the paper. Then have groups each reveal their pentathletes. Have students vote on which team they think would be most likely to win each event in the pentathlon.

Then **ask:**

• **What's difficult about choosing a team to compete in this wide variety of events?**

• **If you were on this team, which events would you like to compete in? not compete in?**

**Say:** It would probably have been easier to choose a team that needed to compete in only one or two of these areas. But when many different things need to be accomplished, it takes many different kinds of people to succeed. If our class were enlisted to compete in this type of event, different people would do well in different events because every person's unique skills would be used in unique ways. Today we'll explore our own uniqueness and the uniqueness of others.

## Warm-Up Option 2

### Pyramid-Building Challenge (up to 15 minutes)

When preteens have arrived, have them form two teams.

Explain to preteens that they will be building human pyramids, based on the descriptions you call out. Explain that after each pyramid is built, three members from each team will switch sides for the next pyramid. Continue switching three members from each team for the remaining pyramid descriptions you call out.

Issue the following challenges: the largest pyramid, the smallest pyramid, a four-sided pyramid, a pyramid of people with the same color socks, a pyramid of all girls, and a pyramid of all guys.

After kids have created their pyramids, **ask:**

• **What was easy about this game? What was hard?**

• **How did switching team members help or hurt your pyramid building efforts?**

**Say:** **For some of these pyramids, some people worked better than others. On other pyramids, other people did better. Trying to build these human structures shows us how different people are. In fact, *every* person is made by God both unique and different from others. Today we're going to see how the variety of people in our world is a good thing, as we explore why ▶ God made each of us unique and different.**

*FYI*

*Whenever groups discuss a list of questions, write the questions on newsprint and tape the newsprint to the wall so groups can discuss the questions at their own pace.*

◀ *The Point*

## Bible Connection

### Body Parts Relay (up to 15 minutes)

Form two teams, the foot team and the eye team. Provide Bibles for each team and have a reader in each team read 1 Corinthians 12:12-20 aloud to his or her team members.

**Say:** **This passage talks about how our hands, feet, eyes, and ears are all needed and important to the proper functioning of our body. Let's play a fun game that will help us explore this idea further.**

Blindfold at least three of the kids in the eye team. Have teams each line up for a relay. Designate a starting line, and place a chair for kids to go around at the other end of the room.

Then **say:** **The first student in each line must walk from the starting line, go around the chair, return to the starting line, and tag the next team member.**

After the relay, the teams will switch. The foot team will become the blind-folded eye team, and we'll run the relay again.

Have teams complete the relay, then switch teams, blindfolding the new "eye" team and repeating the process. After the second relay, have kids gather in their teams.

**Ask:**

• **Which was better in this relay: the eye team or the foot team?**

• **Why was one team better than the other?**

• **How does the Bible passage relate to the two times we ran this relay?**

**Say:** **We held this unusual contest to see how important our eyes were in completing a relay. If one team had its feet tied, it would make the relay pretty hard too. The Bible passage compares our eyes and feet to our talents and abilities. Just as you need your hands, eyes, and feet to allow your body to function well, the Christian body, the church, needs all its members to serve the church body. Let's look at the different ways we can each contribute to a healthy church body.**

*The Point* ➤

### Many People, One Body *(up to 15 minutes)*

Give kids each a photocopy of the "Many People, One Body" handout (p. 13), a pen, and a Bible. Have students complete the handout up to the discussion questions. Then form groups of three or four to compare and discuss the completed handouts.

After a few minutes, have kids form new groups according to their responses to the fill-in-the-blank question on the handout. For example, have all the "eyes" form one group, all the "elbows" form another group, and so on.

**Ask** kids to discuss the following questions in their new groups:

• **Looking around at the new groups, what surprises you most about the way people identify themselves?**

• **How do you feel when you meet someone who isn't like you?**

• **What kinds of people do you have the hardest time getting along with?**

**Say:** **In our group we have some diversity because ➤God made each of us unique and different. But our world is much more diverse. It is filled with smart people, slow thinkers, pretty people, not-so-pretty people, happy people, angry people, and just about everything in between. But as Christians, we**

**each have an important role to play in our church community. Some of you may like to teach younger children, while others may be good at fixing things and can help fix things around church. Others may really like to pray for the sick and hurting. The Bible passage is saying every one of those activities is just as important as the others, and all these things and more contribute to a healthy church body. Let's see how our uniqueness can be used by God.**

## *Life Application*

### Seeking the Unique *(up to 10 minutes)*

Say: ➤**God made each of us unique and different, giving us distinct abilities and experiences. All together these resources can make a winning team out of our class.**

◄ *The Point*

Give each student an index card and a pen. Ask kids to write their names and one positive, unusual thing about themselves. Collect the cards and say: **Our class is full of all kinds of people. Listen to some of the different things that make us special.**

Read the cards aloud saying: **One person is..., another person can do...**

Shuffle the cards and redistribute them to the group. Have kids find the person whose card they hold, and then come up with one way they can encourage that person in his or her special quality. For example, a student could write how he or she appreciates Sarah's care and concern for others and thank her for providing prayer support. Have kids each tell the person what they'll do for encouragement and agree to follow through on that action during the coming week.

Say: **Encouraging other Christians with our words and actions always honors them and pleases God.**

## *Wrap-Up Option 1*

### Getting Along *(up to 5 minutes)*

Give kids each a postcard and a pen. Say: **Think of someone you've had a difficult time accepting lately. What's been the problem? What can you do to resolve the situation and get along with that person? Write a note to that person on your postcard and tell him or her how you feel and what you'll do to get along better. You can send the postcard if you want. Or you may keep it as a reminder to you. Either way you will need to work at accepting this person.**

After a few minutes, have kids form a circle and pray, asking God to give them the confidence to reach out to others who are different from them.

## Wrap-Up Option 2

### Team Appreciation *(up to 10 minutes)*

Form pairs and give each pair a sheet of construction paper, scissors, a marker, and tape. If there is a student without a partner, make one group of three. Have kids each tell their partner one unique way that person contributes to the class. Then have kids each cut out a construction paper "button," write what they said on the button, and tape it to their partner. Encourage kids to take their buttons home as a reminder that their uniqueness is appreciated.

Close by having volunteers pray one-sentence prayers, asking God to help them accept others and appreciate each person's uniqueness.

### Extra-Time Tips

Use these extra ideas to add some creative fun to your studies. They are low-prep or no-prep suggestions that work in no time!

**Variety Counts**—Form groups of no more than four, and have them brainstorm advantages to having variety in a group. See which group can come up with the most advantages.

**Silly Human Tricks**—Have students volunteer to come up front and show the group something unique they can do, such as stand on their head and sing, wiggle their ears, or bend their body like a pretzel. Discuss how kids can use their unique talents to reach out to others.

# Many People, One Body

Read 1 Corinthians 12:20-27, and then summarize it below:

_____

_____

_____

Draw lines from the left column to the right column, matching the body parts with their corresponding personality traits.

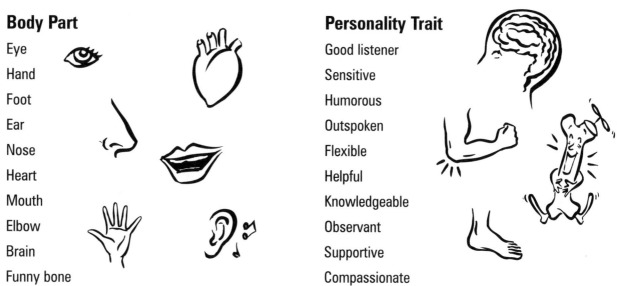

| Body Part | Personality Trait |
|-----------|-------------------|
| Eye | Good listener |
| Hand | Sensitive |
| Foot | Humorous |
| Ear | Outspoken |
| Nose | Flexible |
| Heart | Helpful |
| Mouth | Knowledgeable |
| Elbow | Observant |
| Brain | Supportive |
| Funny bone | Compassionate |

## Discuss the following questions in your small group:

• Pretend someone in your group acted like one of the body parts listed above. How would that person feel? How would others treat him or her?

• The parts of the body contribute to the whole. What are ways different people contribute to your class? What are ways you contribute?

• How do you feel when a member of the class refuses to contribute? when a member is not allowed to contribute?

Fill in the blanks of the following sentence:

The body part that best describes me is _____ because _____.

# A World of People

***The Point:*** ➤ God wants us to reach out to people whom we might see as different.

**M**any preteens live in a melting pot of people from different cultures, with different customs, value systems, and faith perspectives. People from different cultures often are a world apart from a preteen's socioeconomic and relational realm.

Fortunately, we can help preteens break down cultural barriers that hold them back from others. Then they'll be free to effectively carry God's love into all the world.

Use this study to help preteens see the universal needs of all people and cultures and to create a desire to reach out to these people.

## Scripture Source

### Acts 11:1-18

Peter explains his vision from God to the church leaders. He told them that God wanted the Gospel of Christ to be proclaimed to the Gentiles (all non-Jews) throughout the world. Peter tried to convince the Jewish church leaders that they were no longer the exclusive people of God, and that God sent Jesus to all the people of the world.

### Jonah 1:1–2:1; 2:10–3:10

Jonah was a well-known prophet during the time the Assyrian Empire was a major power in the world. Having gained a reputation for ruthlessness and cruelty, the Assyrians were hated by Jonah and other Israelites. So when God told Jonah to reach out to Nineveh, the capital of Assyria, he tried to run away from God's command.

## The Study at a Glance

| Section | Minutes | What Students Will Do | Supplies |
|---|---|---|---|
| **Warm-Up** Option 1 | up to 10 | **A Taste of Something Different**—Try finger foods from all over the world. | Different kinds of foreign finger foods |
| **Warm-Up** Option 2 | up to 10 | **Rapid Immigration**—Play a game about going to other countries. | Masking tape, watch with second hand |
| **Bible Connection** | up to 15 | **Pull-a-Pal**—Pull each other across a boundary line, and then explore Acts 11:1-10. | Bibles, masking tape |
| | up to 20 | **Modern-Day Jonah**—Create and perform skits based on the story of Jonah. | Bibles |
| **Life Application** | up to 10 | **Looking for Nineveh**—Commit to meet the needs of other people. | "Looking for Nineveh" handouts (p. 22), index cards, pens |
| **Wrap-Up** Option 1 | up to 10 | **People Collage**—Create a mural collage of people who are different from them, and then pray for them. | Poster board or newsprint, old magazines showing people of different cultures and backgrounds, glue sticks |
| **Wrap-Up** Option 2 | up to 10 | **If I Were a Foreigner**—Tell where they'd want to go if they could live anywhere. | |

## Before the Study

Set out Bibles, a variety of foreign finger foods (such as Chinese egg rolls, and French pâté), masking tape, watch with second hand, index cards, poster board or newsprint, old magazines showing people of different cultures and backgrounds, glue sticks, and pens. Also make enough photocopies of the "Looking for Nineveh" handout (p. 22) for each preteen.

# The Study

## Warm-Up Option 1

### A Taste of Something Different *(up to 10 minutes)*

Have parents or volunteers prepare different types of finger foods from a variety of countries before the meeting. For example, they might prepare Chinese egg rolls and French pâté on crackers. Or purchase a variety of unusual specialty foods from a local delicatessen or foreign food grocery. Have kids each try at least one item, preferably one they haven't tasted before. After everyone has tasted at least one item, have kids tell what they think of these new foods.

**Ask:** • **How did you feel as you tried something new? Explain.**

• **How is that like the way people feel when they meet someone from another culture or country?**

**Say:** **Sometimes we're afraid to try something new just because it's different. But some of you have found it's worthwhile to try new things. This study will help us see that ▶️God wants us to reach out to people whom we might feel are different from us. Your willingness to try different foods is one way to understand the differences of people in other cultures. Let's explore a culture in the Bible that God's people had a hard time reaching out to.**

◀️ *The Point*

## *Warm-Up Option 2*

### Rapid Immigration *(up to 10 minutes)*

When preteens have arrived, **say:** **Today we're going to explore how ▶️God wants us to reach out to people whom we might feel are different from us. Let's do a fun activity to see what this might be like.**

◀️ *The Point*

Use masking tape or chairs to divide the room into two or three areas or "countries," depending on your room and class size. One country should be sufficient for every five to ten kids. Make the area big enough for all your students to barely fit in. Form the same number of teams as you have countries. Have each team think up a fictional name for its country and reveal it to you.

**Say:** **When I name a country, you're to see how fast you can get within that country's masking tape borders. The people from that country should try to keep others out, but please do it gently. No pushing or shoving. You can stand arm in arm and try to defend your borders, but once someone gets in you can't force him or her out. With my watch, I'll time how long it takes for everyone to get inside the called-out country's borders. Ready?**

When teams are ready, shout "Immigrate to [country's name]!" and have all the kids attempt to get into that country. Time the kids and tell them the result. Call out the remaining countries and have kids repeat the activity, timing each race. After the last immigration race, **ask:**

• **Were some countries harder to get into than others? Why or why not?**

• How was this activity like the way people from different countries try to move to other countries?

• What are some reasons people from other cultures want to immigrate to a new country?

• What are some reasons countries try to keep other people out of their country?

Say: In this activity, we've been pretending to immigrate to other countries. Anytime people move to a new country, both the people immigrating and the people living in that country have to deal with the differences between the people and cultures involved. Today we'll look at a place in the Bible where certain people were different from God's people.

## Bible Connection

### Pull-a-Pal (up to 15 minutes)

Form two teams and have them face each other across a masking tape line on the floor. Tell kids you're going to play a game similar to Tug of War. But the object of this game is for each person to try to pull individual members from the opposing team across the line onto his or her team. Once a player is pulled across the line, he or she must switch teams and start helping the new team win. Remind kids not to be too rough. Play until everyone is on one team.

Ask: • What did you like most about this game?

• What did you like least?

• How did it feel when you were pulled onto the other team's side?

• How is this game like meeting different people? How is it different?

• What were obstacles or boundaries that kept you from pulling people over to your team?

• What are obstacles or boundaries that discourage you from reaching out to people different from you?

Say: Reaching out to people who are different from us is similar to playing this game. At first we were divided, standing on opposing sides of the boundary. But as each person reached out and pulled someone across, we eventually became one team. In a way, this game was like how the early church changed to reach new people in the world. Let's look at this.

Ask a volunteer to read Acts 11:1-10 while kids follow along in their Bibles.

**FYI**

If your class is racially diverse, be sensitive to kids' feelings following this activity. You may discover kids have "obstacles" that keep them from getting along with other class members. If appropriate, discuss kids' feelings and try to help them see the value in breaking down the racial barriers.

**FYI**

Whenever groups discuss a list of questions, write the questions on newsprint and tape the newsprint to the wall so groups can discuss the questions at their own pace.

**Say:** When the church first began, all the people in it were Jews. But God wanted his church ➤to reach out to people of other cultures. His vision to Peter began the church's focus on reaching everyone in the world.

◀ *The Point*

Have another volunteer read Acts 11:11-18 aloud while kids follow along in their Bibles.

**Ask:** • Do you think Peter's explanation to the church leaders is like or unlike how we played our game? Explain.

**Say:** The early church reached out only to God's special people, the Jews. But when the church leaders realized God's desire to tell the people of all cultures about Jesus, they praised God. In another time, one of God's prophets had a very hard time accepting God's love for all people, especially people who were very different from themselves. Let's explore his story.

## Modern-Day Jonah *(up to 20 minutes)*

Read the story of Jonah in Jonah 1:1–2:1 and 2:10–3:10. Then form groups of no more than four. Have the kids in each group create and perform a skit telling this story as if it happened to them instead of Jonah. For example, a group might create a skit in which a student is supposed to reach out to a new foreign-exchange student, but doesn't want to.

As groups design their skits, have them **discuss** these questions:

• **What nation or group of people would you choose as your "Nineveh"?**

• **Where would you run to get away from God?**

• **What would God have to do to get you to obey him?**

When groups are ready, have them perform their skits.

Then **ask:**

• **What did you learn from placing yourself in this story?**

• **What kinds of feelings would you have if God really asked you to do what you demonstrated in the skit? Explain.**

• **How are people today like Jonah?**

• **Which other groups of people do you have to overcome barriers with to reach out to them?**

**Say:** ➤God wants us to reach out to people whom we think are different from us, even people we disagree with. Let's look at how we can apply God's will to our lives.

◀ *The Point*

## Life Application

### Looking for Nineveh (up to 10 minutes)

Give kids each a photocopy of the "Looking for Nineveh" handout (p. 22) and a pen. Have kids complete the handout and then form groups of no more than four.

Have groups **discuss** the following questions:

- **What are the needs of the people in your Nineveh?**

- **How can you help meet these people's needs?**

Form a large circle, and give kids each an index card and a pen. Have kids each write one thing they listed on their handouts that they can do to help meet the needs of the people in their Nineveh. Have kids commit to doing that task during the coming week. When everyone is finished, have kids each tell what they wrote and commit to follow through on their plans.

**Say:** **By reaching out to people from other cultures or in other circumstances, you're pleasing God. Showing God's love to others may be the best opportunity for them to know God loves them.**

## Wrap-Up Option 1

### People Collage (up to 10 minutes)

Have preteens form groups of up to four. Provide them with old magazines, glue sticks, and poster board. **Say:** **We've been looking at people who are different from us in a variety of ways. I want you to go through these magazines and tear out pictures of people who you would describe as different from you. Work in your groups to create a people collage.**

Give groups about five to eight minutes to complete their collages.

**Ask:** **• How can your collage encourage you to reach out to people who are different from you?**

Place the collages together on a table or the floor and have preteens gather around them. Close in prayer, asking God to help kids reach out to everyone in his name.

## Wrap-Up Option 2

### If I Were a Foreigner (up to 10 minutes)

Form pairs. Ask students to share with one another which country they would want to live in if they could live anywhere. Also have partners explain why they want to live there.

Close by having kids tell their partners one positive thing they each would bring to any nation they moved to. For example, someone might say, "You could bring happiness to the people of this country" or "Your intelligence could help this nation succeed in business."

Have kids pray for their partners that God would use them to reach out to people both here and far away.

## Extra-Time Tips

Use these extra ideas to add some creative fun to your studies. They are low-prep or no-prep concepts that can work well for you!

**To Move or Not to Move**—Challenge the students to determine the pros and cons of moving to another country. Have kids discuss what it would take to adapt to another culture.

**Over the Sea**—Have kids tell of trips they or their friends have taken to other countries. Ask kids to tell what went right and what didn't go right about the trips. Encourage them to identify lessons they learned from their experiences.

# LOOKING for NINEVEH

When Jonah began running away from God, he was looking for a way to escape going to Nineveh. Eventually, however, Jonah discovered God was right in leading him to this other land.

What is your "Nineveh"? Which culture, country, group, or type of people do you have the most difficult time reaching out to? In the space on the map, write this Nineveh. Then list three things you can do to follow God's will and reach out to these people in a positive way. You'll be sharing one of these ideas with the whole group.

## My Nineveh

1.

2.

3.

# Overcoming Racism and Prejudice

***The Point:*** ➤ God warns us that racism and prejudice are harmful attitudes and actions.

Racist statements have been used to put down people of all kinds. Although we wish it weren't so, racism and prejudice still exist among preteens. Many kids try to deal with their own sinking self-esteem and insecurity by degrading others. However, through Christ we can help kids learn about the pain of prejudice and the value of love.

Jesus and Paul made it clear that prejudicial attitudes and actions are not acceptable behaviors in God's sight. Use this study to help preteens explore how to show love to those who are different from themselves.

## Scripture Source

### Luke 10:30-37

Jesus told the story of the good Samaritan in response to the question, "Who is my neighbor?" The Jewish people Jesus spoke to were guilty of racism and prejudice toward the "half-blooded" Samaritans. Yet Jesus made the Samaritan the hero of the story. Jesus pointed out that we should be neighbors to all people, regardless of their race or culture.

### Colossians 3:11

Paul makes it clear that in Christ there is no distinction based on race or social status. Paul taught that because we're all equal before God, we should treat each other with compassion and kindness, just as God has treated us.

## The Study at a Glance

| Section | Minutes | What Students Will Do | Supplies |
|---------|---------|----------------------|----------|
| **Warm-Up** Option 1 | up to 10 | **Addition/Subtraction**—Add and subtract points for a competition based on things out of their control. | Paper, pens |
| **Warm-Up** Option 2 | up to 10 | **Musical Clusters**—Form groups of varying size based on the leader's whim. | CD of background music, CD player |
| **Bible Connection** | up to 15 | **Biased Bible Game**—Play a Bible trivia game that is obviously biased toward one team, and then compare the game to Colossians 3:11. | Bibles, "Bible Time Q & A" handouts (p. 32), pens |
| | up to 20 | **Beyond Racism**—Act out the story of the good Samaritan and explore Luke 10:30-37. | Bibles, "The Good Samaritan" handout (p. 33), "Applause" and "Boo" signs, newsprint, marker, paper, pens |
| **Life Application** | up to 10 | **Left Is Right and Right Is Wrong**—Write situations where people experience prejudice, and write ways to combat prejudice. | Tape, newsprint, markers, index cards, pens |
| **Wrap-Up** Option 1 | up to 5 | **Justice Prayer**—List parts of an anti-prejudice prayer, and pray it as a responsive prayer. | Newsprint, markers |
| **Wrap-Up** Option 2 | up to 10 | **If People Were Money**—Observe a demonstration emphasizing their value to God. | "People Money" handout (p. 32), pens, scissors |

## Before the Study

Set out Bibles, a CD of background music, CD player, writing paper, markers, index cards, tape, newsprint, pens, and scissors. You'll need to make two signs that say "Applause" and "Boo." You'll need three photocopies of "The Good Samaritan" handout (p. 33). Also make enough photocopies of the "Bible Time Q &A/People Money" handout (p. 32) for each preteen to have one, plus one for the leader.

# The Study

## Warm-Up Option 1

### Addition/Subtraction *(up to 10 minutes)*

**The Point ➤** When preteens have arrived, **say: Today we're going to explore how ➤God warns us that racism and prejudice are harmful attitudes and actions. Let's play a game to see how this is so.**

*24 • Getting Along With Others*

Give each person a sheet of paper and a pen. Tell kids you're going to play a scoring game. Give kids each 100 points to start with, and say that the person with the most points at the end of the game wins. **Read** aloud the following list and have students add and subtract points as you go:

**Subtract 8 points if you are a girl.**

**Subtract 7 points if you are taller than your mother.**

**Subtract 15 points if you don't have any cavities.**

**Add 10 points if you wear braces.**

**Add 9 points if you wear glasses.**

**Subtract 10 points if you are involved in sports.**

**Add 4 points if you had to change schools during the year.**

**Subtract 5 points if you are in the school band.**

**Add 13 points if you have 10 dollars or more with you.**

**Subtract 12 points if you didn't go on a vacation last year.**

**Add 7 points if you're carrying a brush or comb.**

**Subtract 50 points if you currently have 70 or fewer points.**

After determining who has the most points, **ask:**

• **How did you feel during this competition?**

• **How is that like or unlike the way people who are victims of prejudice might feel? Explain.**

• **Was this competition fair? Why or why not?**

**Say:** **You might feel that you lost points for reasons that weren't fair. If you do, you're right. This study will help us see that sometimes we make unfair judgments about people. Let's explore what the Bible has to say about this.**

## Warm-Up Option 2

### Musical Clusters *(up to 10 minutes)*

When preteens have arrived, **say:** **Today we're going to explore how ➤God**  ◀ **The Point**
**warns us that racism and prejudice are harmful attitudes and actions. Let's do an activity to see what this feels like.**

Have students mill about the room while music is playing. When you stop the music, shout out a number between one and six. Have group members try to form "clusters" of exactly that many people. For example, if you call out "four," kids should gather into groups of four. Any who aren't able to join a cluster should sit down.

After several rounds, **ask:**

- **How did you feel when you were left out of a group?**

- **How is that like the way people feel when they're left out of an activity because of their race or another factor?**

**Say:** **In this activity, you may have pushed others out of your cluster so that you would have the right number to win. Or you may have been pushed out of a cluster just because there was one person too many. That's unfair! Today we're going to focus on how people are excluded sometimes simply because others are close-minded about letting new people in. Let's explore what the Bible has to say about this.**

## *Bible Connection*

### Biased Bible Game *(up to 15 minutes)*

Before this study photocopy the "Bible Time Q & A"/People Money" handout (p. 32). You'll need one copy for each student. Cut the "People Money" section off for use later in the study. Then cut the "Bible Time Q & A" page into two halves, stacking the "Team A Questions" into one pile and the "Team B Questions" into another.

Form two teams based on kids' birthdays. Team A should be those people born January through June. Team B should be those born July through December. It's OK to have uneven numbers, but if the teams are quite unbalanced, add a few members from the larger team to balance out the teams a bit.

**Say:** **Welcome to Bible Time Q and A, the game show where contestants read both the questions and the answers. But will you read the *correct* answers? That's why I'm here. I have the correct answers. You may talk among your team members until I ask you for the answer to each of the questions. Ready? Let's play!**

Distribute the Bible Time Q & A slips to the respective teams. Team A has very hard questions, and it is unlikely they will know any of their answers, while Team B should know the answers to their easy questions.

Have Team A read their first question aloud and give them about ten seconds to answer. Announce the answer after time is up, and then have Team B read their first question. Give them about ten seconds (if necessary) before giving their answer. Repeat this sequence on the remaining four questions for each team.

**Team A Questions and Answers:**

**Question 1:** In the Bible, who is called the "Queen of Heaven"?

**Answer 1:** a pagan goddess referenced in Jeremiah 7:18

**Question 2:** Under which empire did Ezekiel prophesy?

**Answer 2:** Babylonian (Ezekiel 1:2)

**Question 3:** Where did Moses' sister Miriam die?

**Answer 3:** Kadesh (Numbers 20:1)

**Question 4:** When Israel's enemies outnumbered them, what plant did Asaph say God would make the enemies like?

**Answer 4:** Tumbleweed (Psalm 83:13)

**Question 5:** What is Mt. Hermon called by the Sidonians?

**Answer 5:** Sirion (Deuteronomy 3:9)


**Team B Questions and Answers:**

**Question 1:** What is the first book in the Bible?

**Answer 1:** Genesis

**Question 2:** What did Noah build before the floods came?

**Answer 2:** The ark (Genesis 6)

**Question 3:** Who was Adam's mate?

**Answer 3:** Eve (Genesis 2)

**Question 4:** Who was the mother of the baby Jesus?

**Answer 4:** Mary (Matthew 2)

**Question 5:** On what object was Jesus crucified?

**Answer 5:** a cross (Mark 15)


After the game, **ask:**

- **How did it feel to be a part of team A?**
- **How did it feel to be on team B?**
- **What did you want to do when you figured out the game was being played unfairly?**

Provide Bibles to each team and have preteens look up Colossians 3:11. Ask a member on Team A to read the passage aloud to the whole group.

**Ask:** • **What do you think this passage is talking about?**

- **How does this passage relate to how our Bible trivia game was played?**

**Say:** I have to admit this game was rigged. I deliberately gave team A very hard questions, whose answers even I didn't know. Team B got very easy questions. I was prejudiced against Team A by making it impossible for them to win the game. But in real life being prejudiced toward someone for the color of their skin, or their nationality, or their religion is a serious issue. Let's

*The Point* ➤ explore a very interesting story Jesus told about why ➤racism and prejudice are harmful attitudes and actions.

### Beyond Racism (up to 20 minutes)

**Say:** One group of New Testament people that was often treated unfairly was the Samaritans. The Jews hated them because Samaritan people were descended from a mixture of Jews and Gentiles (non-Jews). As a result, they were looked down upon and ridiculed for not being as "good" as the Jewish people. However, Jesus saw them in a different light. Let's take a look at a story he told about a Samaritan.

Ask for volunteers to act out the story of the good Samaritan in Luke 10:30-37. You'll need a narrator, a traveler, a couple of robbers, a priest, a Levite, a Samaritan, a donkey, and an innkeeper. Also select two students who will hold up signs saying "Applause" and "Boo" as cue cards for the remaining students (or students who currently aren't acting). It's OK for kids to play more than one role if your group is smaller than ten. Provide the narrator and the two sign-holders photocopies of "The Good Samaritan" script handout (p. 33). Have the narrator read the story, pausing to give actors enough time to mime the actions. Also have the narrator pause when the script calls for the "Applause" and "Boo" kids to parade their signs across the stage.

After the story, **ask:**

• How would you have felt if you were the man on the side of the road?

• Why do you think the priest and the Levite passed by?

• Why do you think the Samaritan stopped to help someone who was probably a Jew, who supposedly hated Samaritans?

• How are the people in this story like people we know today?

**Say:** People still hate others because of race, just as they did back in New Testament days. But prejudice goes beyond racism alone. We can be prejudiced against the rich, the talented, or the beautiful people. Let's discover some other groups that may experience prejudice today.

Brainstorm with kids the different types of crowds or cliques at their schools, such as video gamers, athletes, snobs, rich kids, and fashion followers. Write the lists on newsprint with a marker.

**Say:** **Let's revisit a Bible passage we read earlier to see how it might apply to these lists of people.**

Ask a volunteer to read Colossians 3:11 aloud. After reading the verse, give kids a sheet of paper and a pen. Have kids act as ghostwriters and rewrite the passage the way Paul might have written it if he'd had these new contemporary classifications of people in mind. Have volunteers read their rewritten verses to the whole group.

Then **ask:**

• **How do you think Paul would respond to the prejudice in your school?**

• **How can you respond to it?**

• **How do you think God feels about racism and prejudice?**

**Say:** **Prejudice is hard to ignore when it affects you directly. But it can be easy to overlook when it's aimed at someone else. Yet prejudice will come to an end only when you and I do what we can to stay free from it and help others overcome it too.**

## *Life Application*

### Left Is Right and Right Is Wrong *(up to 10 minutes)*

**Say:** ▶**God warns us that racism and prejudice are harmful attitudes and actions. Let's see how we can avoid them.**

◀ *The Point*

Tape a large sheet of newsprint on the wall on the right side of the room. Ask students each to write on the newsprint a brief school situation where someone might feel the pain of racism or prejudice. For example, someone might write, "A new kid with braces joins band, and kids make fun of him."

Then, on another sheet of newsprint taped on the left side of the room, have kids each write ways they can combat racism and prejudice at their school based on both the situations listed on the first sheet of newsprint and other experiences they have had.

Give kids each an index card and a pen. Have kids each choose one of the ideas from the newsprint on the left side of the room and write it on the card as a commitment to do this at school during the coming month.

*FYI*

*Whenever groups discuss a list of questions, write the questions on newsprint and tape the newsprint to the wall so groups can discuss the questions at their own pace.*

**Say:** Take your index card home and tape it to your bathroom mirror as a reminder of your commitment this month. Every effort you make will help your school and the world become a little more free from racism and prejudice.

## Wrap-Up Option 1

### Justice Prayer *(up to 5 minutes)*

**Say:** The word *prejudice* means prejudging someone based on factors the person cannot change, such as his or her race. Today we've learned how

**The Point** ➤ ➤racism and prejudice are harmful. God encourages Christians to practice justice. Let's do that now by listing things you would like to contribute to prayer. After we've listed everything, we'll go around in a circle and pray the parts of the justice prayer we create.

List kids' responses on a sheet of newsprint with a marker. Then have kids gather in a semicircle around the list, and have kids read their portion of the prayer aloud. Close the prayer by thanking God for the point of the study and asking for strength to live nonprejudicial lives.

## Wrap-Up Option 2

### If People Were Money *(up to 10 minutes)*

Hold up a bill cut out from the photocopy of the "People Money" handout (p. 32). **Say:** This is a six billion bill. But it's not six billion dollars; it's called a People Money bill because there are more than six billion people in the world. This bill represents all the people in the world. When we give in to racism and prejudice, it's like tearing apart God's treasured creation.

Tear off a section of the bill and **say:** At first the bill may still be usable, even though the corner is torn off. But then as more pieces are torn off (tear off more pieces), **as more people give in to prejudice and racism, the whole bill loses its purpose and its value.**

Hold out the shredded people bill for kids to see. Then give preteens a photocopy of the "People Money" handout and scissors. Have kids cut apart the handout to form two bills. Then have them form pairs or trios. Ask kids each to write one way their partner adds to God's "treasure" on one of the bills. Then have kids exchange bills while telling their partners what they wrote.

Then **say: Having loving attitudes and actions toward others is one way to overcome racism and prejudice. On your second bill, write down a group of people toward which you might struggle to show loving attitudes and actions. Take this home as a reminder not to give in to the destructive power of prejudice. Let this six billion people bill remind you that we all need each other, regardless of race or other differences.**

Close with prayer, asking God to help kids fight prejudice wherever they find it in their lives.

### Extra-Time Tips

Use these extra ideas to add some creative fun to your studies. They are low-prep or no-prep activities that work in no time!

**If God Came Today**—Have kids discuss what Jesus might be like if he came today instead of 2,000 years ago. Which race would he be? What clubs would he belong to? Who would be his best friends? Who would be his enemies? How would other people treat him?

**We're All Gray**—Give each person a sheet of gray paper. Have kids punch out "eye" and "mouth" holes in the papers and hold them up as if wearing masks. While kids wear their masks, have them discuss what the world would be like if everyone looked alike. Encourage kids to explore the value of varied cultures and races and what they can learn from people who are different from them.

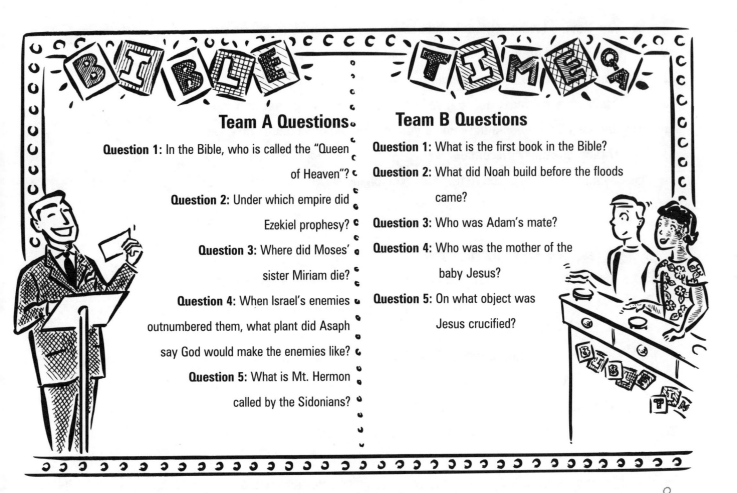

## Team A Questions

**Question 1:** In the Bible, who is called the "Queen of Heaven"?

**Question 2:** Under which empire did Ezekiel prophesy?

**Question 3:** Where did Moses' sister Miriam die?

**Question 4:** When Israel's enemies outnumbered them, what plant did Asaph say God would make the enemies like?

**Question 5:** What is Mt. Hermon called by the Sidonians?

## Team B Questions

**Question 1:** What is the first book in the Bible?

**Question 2:** What did Noah build before the floods came?

**Question 3:** Who was Adam's mate?

**Question 4:** Who was the mother of the baby Jesus?

**Question 5:** On what object was Jesus crucified?

# People Money

# The Good Samaritan

*Based on Luke 10:30-37*

A man was going down from Jerusalem to Jericho *(applause)* when he fell into the hands of robbers *(boo)*. They stripped him of his clothes, beat him, and went away leaving him half dead *(boo)*. A priest, well-respected and very religious, happened to be going down the same road *(applause)*, and when he saw the man, he passed by on the other side *(boo)*.

So, too, a Levite, who came from a good and influential family, was going down the road *(applause)*. When he came to the place and saw the man, he passed by on the other side *(boo)*. But a Samaritan, one who was disliked by the Jews, also came by. He had been treated poorly by Jewish people in the past because he was from Samaria.

However, as he traveled, the Samaritan came to where the man was, and when he saw him, he took pity on him *(applause)*. He went to him and bandaged his wounds *(applause)*. Then he put the man on his own donkey, took him to an inn, and took care of him *(applause)*. The next day, he took out two silver coins and gave them to the innkeeper. "Look after him," he said, "and when I return, I will reimburse you for any extra expense you may have" *(applause)*.

# Same Church, Different Building

*The Point:* ➤ All Christians fit into the big picture of the "church."

hurch history is full of division, backbiting, and bitter struggles to assert denominational or sectarian superiority. Selfish attitudes and intolerance of others whose beliefs or church traditions are different have created numerous divisions among Christians. Sadly, preteens are as susceptible to divisive attitudes as Christians of the past were.

God, however, has something much better in store for young people: Christian unity. Although Christians are represented in churches of many denominations, believers are all part of God's worldwide "body of Christ." Understanding this can empower kids to change their world for the better.

## Scripture Source

### Ephesians 4:1-7

Paul urges Christians to keep the unity of the Spirit in peace with each other. He emphasizes God's desire for unity among his children. Just as we are all part of the same body and serving the same Lord, we should strive to live together in peace.

### Ephesians 4:11-13

Paul explains that the variety of natural abilities and spiritual gifts among church leaders is for building up the body of Christ as a whole. Christians are to strive to be unified in the Spirit and to become mature believers.

## The Study at a Glance

| Section | Minutes | What Students Will Do | Supplies |
|---|---|---|---|
| **Warm-Up** Option 1 | up to 10 | **Silent Church**—Mime actions that indicate what church means to them. | |
| **Warm-Up** Option 2 | up to 5 | **Invisible Phone Booth**—Fit as many people as possible into a square marked on the floor. | Masking tape |
| **Bible Connection** | up to 15 | **Drawing Conclusions**—Draw pictures based on Ephesians 4:1-7, and then discuss how their pictures are different. | Bibles, newsprint, markers |
| | up to 25 | **Shoe Churches**—Debate shoe type merits, experience separation, then explore church leadership roles in Ephesians 4:11-13. | Bibles, chairs or sheets |
| **Life Application** | up to 15 | **How to Treat Royalty**—Explore how they would treat a famous person. | Bibles, "How to Treat Royalty" handouts (p. 42), pens |
| **Wrap-Up** Option 1 | up to 5 | **Song of Unity**—Sing about Christian unity. | Hymnals or songbooks |
| **Wrap-Up** Option 2 | up to 5 | **A Piece of the Puzzle**—Compare Christian unity to a puzzle. | A 500-piece puzzle |

## Before the Study

Set out Bibles, chairs or sheets, masking tape, newsprint, markers, pens, hymnals or songbooks, and a puzzle. Also make enough photocopies of the "How to Treat Royalty" handout (p. 42) for each preteen.

**Note:** In this study, you'll need to distinguish between Christian denominations and other religions. Denominations are associations of Christian churches with identifying names such as Baptist, Methodist, and Assemblies of God. Though different in many respects, they all hold to basic beliefs about Jesus Christ.

Beyond these are other religions, which include Islam and Jehovah's Witnesses. These groups do not hold to the fundamental beliefs about Christ and his deity and are not considered Christian. When speaking about Christian unity, make sure your students are aware that you are speaking about Christian denominations and not all religions.

# The Study

## Warm-Up Option 1

### Silent Church (up to 10 minutes)

After preteens arrive, **say: Today we'll be talking about the church. To begin, I would like you to consider what comes to mind when I say the word *church* to you.**

Have kids form groups of three or four, and have each group discuss things that happen at church, such as listening to the pastor give a sermon or babies being cared for in a nursery. Have groups decide on one activity, then create a mime (silent acting) to perform for the larger group. Give groups about two minutes to prepare their mimes. Then have groups make their presentations while having class members try to guess what they are doing. After all groups have presented, **ask:**

- **Was it easy or hard to create mimes of church activities? Explain.**
- **Why did your group choose the activity it did to mime?**

**Say: The activities we presented show we have a lot of different ideas of church. Just as each group chose a differemt activity relating to church, there are many Christian churches with different ideas about what it means to follow God. Today we'll discover how ▶all Christians fit into the big picture of the "church."**

◀ *The Point*

## Warm-Up Option 2

### Invisible Phone Booth (up to 5 minutes)

Using masking tape, make several squares on the floor (about two feet square). Form groups of no more than ten. Have groups each try to fit as many people as they can inside the square they have been given without anyone touching the floor outside of the square.

Allow several tries, and applaud the group that gets the most people inside its square.

Then **ask:**

- **How easy was it to get everyone into the square?**
- **How did you work together in the activity?**

**Say: In this activity, you really had to work together as a team. The people**

in God's church also need to work together to accomplish his will in the world. Today we're going to talk about who is part of the Christian church as we discover how ➤all Christians fit into the big picture of the "church."

*The Point* ➤

## *Bible Connection*

### Drawing Conclusions (up to 15 minutes)

Say: Let's see what the Bible has to say about unity among Christians.

Form groups of no more than four. Give each group a sheet of newsprint, markers, and a Bible. Have groups each read Ephesians 4:1-7 and then draw a poster that illustrates the passage in some way.

When groups are finished, have them explain their illustrations. Then ask:

• What made you decide to illustrate the passage in this way?

Say: Look around at the other illustrations. They aren't like yours, even though they illustrate the same passage.

Then ask:

• Are the other illustrations wrong? Why or why not?

• How is that like different denominations in the Christian faith?

Say: Just as each of your pictures illustrates the same passage individually, so each Christian denomination illustrates the truth of the Gospel in its particular way. We can see from this experience that the denominations can be different and yet all follow God. Let's explore this idea further.

### Shoe Churches (up to 25 minutes)

Have kids remove their shoes and place them into one of the following piles: white tennis shoes, colored tennis shoes, sandals, loafers, and other types of footwear. Place the piles in various locations in the room.

Have students stand next to the pile of shoes they think is the best type of shoe. Then have groups defend their choices by explaining why their shoes are best and why the others are inferior. Encourage groups to huddle together and become more adamant about their choices as they defend their favorite shoe styles.

As the debate heats up, begin to separate the groups by putting chairs between them or, if possible, hanging sheets from the ceiling between them. After a few minutes, each group should be totally separated from the other groups.

**Ask:**

• How does it feel to be separated from the other groups?

• How is the way groups were divided over their favorite shoe styles like or unlike the way church groups are separated because of different teachings or traditions? Explain.

• How did it feel to have to choose only one type of shoe?

• What would life be like if we could own only one pair of shoes?

• How are the different groups of shoes like different Christian churches?

• How would you feel if everybody had to believe exactly the same things to go to church?

• How is the need for different types of shoes like the need for different kinds of Christian churches?

**Say:** Although the shoes individually belong to different groups, we need them all to complete the "family" of shoes. Likewise, Christians belong to many different churches, but they are all needed to complete the family of God.

**Ask:** • What is the purpose of shoes?

**Say:** It seems pretty obvious what shoes are for. They protect and keep our feet warm, among other things.

**Ask:** • What is the purpose of the church?

**Say:** It may also seem pretty obvious the church is where people learn about following Jesus and God. But let's look at a Bible passage that gives us an idea of how different churches teach or share Jesus in different ways.

Ask a volunteer read Ephesians 4:11-13 aloud to the whole group. Then have kids form five groups. Assign one of the leadership roles listed in Ephesians 4:11-13 to each group. Give preteens a few minutes to brainstorm what they think these leadership roles are. Then have groups share their ideas. As they do so, ask other groups if they have a different understanding of these roles. After groups have shared and discussed all five roles, **say:** Just as our shoes, which represented churches have a variety in appearance and uses, God has given churches different leaders to teach Christians how to serve in different ways. Some churches focus mostly on evangelism by sending missionaries to nations whose people generally don't know Jesus. Other churches show compassion and concern for the poor, homeless, and suffering people in their city. Still other churches do both these things and more. The leadership gifts involved in these godly pursuits help ➤ all Christians fit into the big picture of the "church."

## *Life Application*

### How to Treat Royalty (up to 15 minutes)

Say: Now that we know all Christians everywhere are part of the same faith, let's think about how that knowledge should change the way we live. To do this, let's pretend we're going to have a very important person over for an evening meal.

Give students each a photocopy of the "How to Treat Royalty" handout (p. 42) and a pen. Have kids complete their handouts. When everyone is finished, tell kids to cross out the word *Royalty* from the title of their handouts and write in the word *Christians.*

Read aloud 1 Peter 2:9 and then say: Since all Christians are part of God's family, then we're all VIPs (very important persons). And we need to treat other Christians, whoever they are, with the honor they deserve.

Have kids sign their names at the bottom of their handouts as a sign of their commitment to treat other Christians with honor and to strive for unity in Christ's church. Then have kids each start living out their commitment by turning to the person on their right and telling him or her one "royal" quality that makes that person special to God. For example, someone might say, "You have the royal quality of concern for others."

Encourage students to take their handouts home to remind them of their commitments.

## *Wrap-Up Option 1*

### Song of Unity (up to 5 minutes)

Say: We've learned today, in Christ, we truly are bonded together in unity. Let's celebrate that unity by singing a song together.

Have students stand and hold hands in a circle. Sing "They'll Know We Are Christians by Our Love" or another song about Christian unity. When the song is over, point out how each person's voice added a unique quality to the song that it wouldn't have had if that person had not participated.

Then close by reading or reciting an appropriate verse of the song as a closing prayer.

## Wrap-Up Option 2

### A Piece of the Puzzle (up to 5 minutes)

Show the group a 500-piece jigsaw puzzle. **Say: Sometimes the church looks to us like a jumbled mess of puzzle pieces.**

Show the top of the puzzle box with its picture of the completed puzzle. **Say: God knows what a beautiful picture our church can make. We're all pieces in his puzzle, and he knows how all of the pieces fit together.**

Close with prayer, asking God to build unity in his body all over the world. After the prayer, dump the puzzle pieces onto a table for kids to work on after class or during the coming weeks.

## Extra-Time Tips

Use these extra ideas to add some creative fun to your studies. They are low-prep or no-prep ideas that work in no time!

**Never-Ending Story**—As an illustration of how God uses other Christians to add to our lives, have the students play Never-Ending Story. Begin by making up a story and then point to a group member to pick up the story where you left off. Have the student continue the story for a minute or so, and then interrupt him or her and select another group member to pick up the story. Continue until the story ends or time is up. Discuss how each person added to the story and how each Christian adds to the story of God's people.

**A Different Perspective**—Arrange to have a pastor or teacher from a church of another denomination present a summary of his or her church's teachings and traditions. Encourage kids to ask questions. Be sure to check with your church leadership about your intentions, before inviting a guest.

# HOW TO TREAT ROYALTY

*Imagine you will have as a guest for an evening one of the following people: the queen of England, the president of the United States, or a movie star. Then, in the chart, write your answers to the following questions about your evening.*

| Questions | Queen | President | Star |
|---|---|---|---|
| How would you feel about entertaining this person? Explain. | | | |
| What would you serve for dinner? | | | |
| How would you dress? | | | |
| How would you prepare for his or her arrival? | | | |
| What would you talk about? | | | |
| After the guest left, how would you like him or her to remember you? Explain. | | | |

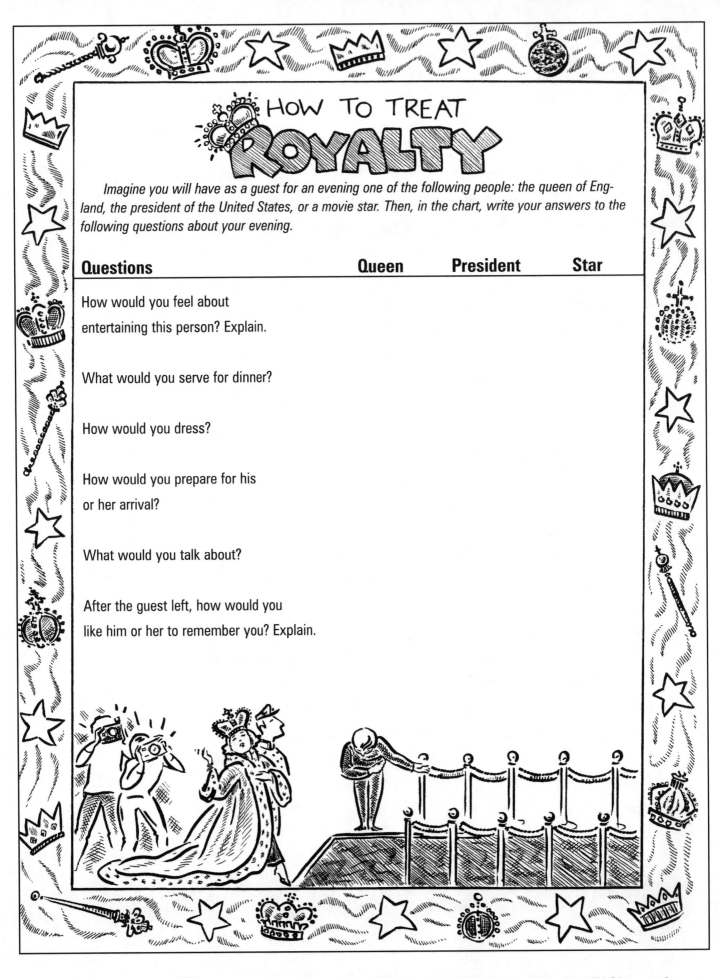

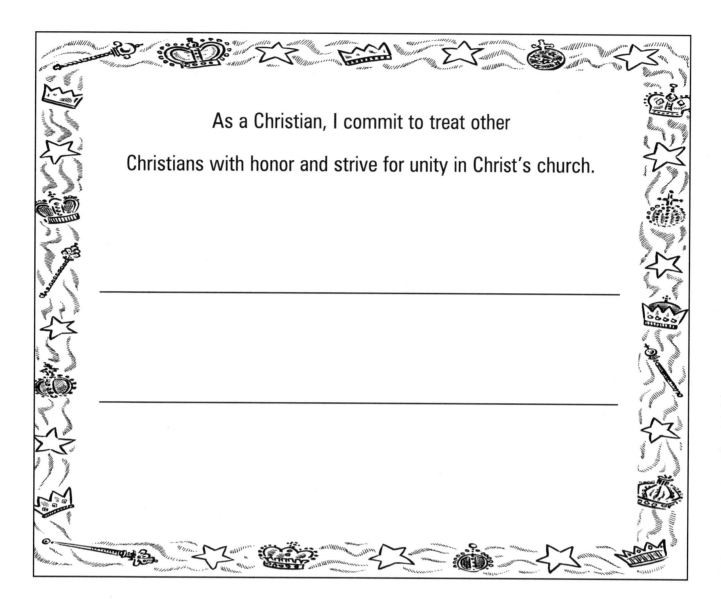

As a Christian, I commit to treat other

Christians with honor and strive for unity in Christ's church.

_____

_____

To make the impact of these Bible studies last far beyond their conclusion, try this idea. Conduct a retreat that explores a missionary lifestyle both in the United States and abroad. Invite as guest speakers one person who has been a missionary overseas and another who has been involved in mission work in the United States. Use Acts 1:8 as your theme for the weekend.

For fun, take everyone's pictures before you leave and make "passports" to be used during the retreat. Encourage the kids to carry them at all times. Require them to be shown at mealtimes and award special surprises to students who are able to produce them upon request throughout the day.

Group Publishing, Inc.
Attention: Product Development
P.O. Box 481
Loveland, CO 80539
Fax: (970) 679-4370

# Evaluation for
## *Getting Along With Others*
## *(Faith 4 Life: Preteen Bible Study Series)*

Please help Group Publishing, Inc., continue to provide innovative and useful resources for ministry. Please take a moment to fill out this evaluation and mail or fax it to us. Thanks!

● ● ●

1. As a whole, this book has been (circle one)

not very helpful                                              very helpful

1      2      3      4      5      6      7      8      9      10


2. The best things about this book:


3. Ways this book could be improved:


4. Things I will change because of this book:


5. Other books I'd like to see Group publish in the future:


6. Would you be interested in field-testing future Group products and giving us
   your feedback? If so, please fill in the information below:

Name _____

Church Name _____

Denomination _____ Church Size _____

Church Address _____

City _____ State _____ ZIP _____

Church Phone _____

E-mail _____

# Look for the Whole Family of Faith 4 Life Bible Studies!

## Preteen Books
**Being Responsible**
**Getting Along With Others**

**God in My Life**
**Going Through Tough Times**

## Junior High Books
**Becoming a Christian**
**Finding Your Identity**

**God's Purpose for Me**
**Understanding the Bible**

## Senior High Books
**Family Matters**
**Is There Life After High School?**

**Prayer**
**Sharing Your Faith**

# Coming Soon...

## For Preteens
**Building Friendships**
**Handling Conflict**
**How to Make Great Choices**
**Peer Pressure**

**Succeeding in School**
**The Bible and Me**
**What's a Christian?**
**Why God Made Me**

## For Junior High
**Choosing Wisely**
**Fighting Temptation**
**Friends**
**How to Pray**

**My Family Life**
**My Life as a Christian**
**Sharing Jesus**
**Who Is God?**

## For Senior High
**Applying God's Word**
**Believing in Jesus**
**Christian Character**
**Following Jesus**

**Sexuality**
**Worshipping 24/7**
**Your Christian ID**
**Your Relationships**

Visit your local Christian bookstore or contact Group Publishing, Inc., at 800-447-1070. www.grouppublishing.com

# More Preteen Ministry Resources!

## The Preteen Worker's Encyclopedia of Bible-Teaching Ideas

Make the New Testament come alive to your preteens and help them discover Bible truths in a big way! In this comprehensive collection, you get nearly 200 creative ideas and activities including: object lessons, skits, games, devotions, service projects, creative prayers, affirmations, creative readings, retreats, parties, trips and travel, and music ideas.

Flexible for any group setting, you'll easily find the perfect idea with helpful Scripture and theme indexes.

**ISBN 0-7644-2425-4**

## Dynamic Preteen Ministry

*Gordon West & Becki West*

Maximize ministry to preteens as they make the difficult transition from childhood to adolescence. Both children's and youth workers will better understand the minds and emotions of 10- to 14-year-olds, "bridge the gap" between children's ministry and youth ministry.

**ISBN 0-7644-2084-4**

## No-Miss Lessons for Preteen Kids

Here are 22 faith-building lessons that keep 5th- and 6th-graders coming back! Children's workers get active-learning lessons dealing with faith…self-esteem…relationships…choices…and age-appropriate service projects that any preteen class can do!

**ISBN 0-7644-2015-1**

## No-Miss Lessons for Preteen Kids 2

Enjoy ministering to your preteens like never before! This flexible resource features 20 action-packed, easy-to-teach lessons that talk about the stuff of life in the preteen world. Stuff like the Internet and media, how to get along with family and friends, faith foundations based on God and Jesus, and many others! These lessons and the 13 bonus, "can't-miss" service project ideas will challenge kids, grow their faith, and give them practical ideas for living out their deepening faith in meaningful ways!

**ISBN 0-7644-2290-1**

# More Preteen Ministry Resources!

*(continued)*

## The Ultimate Book of Preteen Games

They're not children. Not teenagers. What do you do with preteens? Have a blast! Start with these 100 games they'll love! In the process, you'll break down cliques, build relationships, explore relevant Bible truths, give thought-provoking challenges, and have high-energy fun!

**0-7644-2291-X**

## Emotion Explosion!: 40 Devotions for Preteen Ministry

*Carol Mader*

Show preteens that God understands their confusing emotions and cares about how they feel. With these 40 fun devotions based on the Psalms, preteens will explore the highs and lows of the life of David, and learn to take their feelings of doubt and sorrow, hope and joy to God. Group games and activities make this the perfect devotional for preteens.

Reproducibles included!

**ISBN 0-7644-2221-9**

Order today from your local Christian bookstore, online at www.faithweaver.com or write:
Group Publishing, P.O. Box 485, Loveland, CO 80539-0485.